Documentary Media
Seattle Washington

PROCESS
seattle central library

Lara Swimmer

Contents

FOREWORD

The opening of this remarkable Central Library for the Seattle Public Library system marks an important chapter in the cultural development of the Pacific Northwest. Indeed, it is the culmination of two decades of massive building for the arts.

During this period we have created facilities for theater, music, dance, and the visual arts as well as overseen the renovation of schools for the teaching of the arts. Within this region, over one and a half billion dollars has been spent on capital projects designed by professionals to meet the needs of the creative activities that happen within them.

The Rem Koolhaas-designed library is a symbolic testimony of our commitment to education and culture, a state-of-the-art repository of the ideas we value as a community and as a people. It is fitting that it is the final and most ambitious structure of an extraordinary period of cultural building.

The process of the structure's evolution, as captured in these pages by the photography of Lara Swimmer, in many ways mirrors Seattle's evolution in its support of the arts and education. It took vision as well as personal and community commitment. Its comprehensive form is the product of many interconnected and linked achievements.

In its final form, the Central Library is a testament to the evolution Seattle has undergone and an inspiration as we look to the future.

Peter Donnelly, President & CEO, ArtsFund, Seattle

INTRODUCTION

The new library, unlike any building seen before in Seattle, will become many things to many people: research facility, gathering place, sanctuary, communications center, architectural wonder, cultural artifact. But it is also an entity in its own right, an edifice whose raw internal complexity helps to explain the strength of its presence in our midst.

In capturing candid moments of the library's process of becoming, photographer Lara Swimmer provides us a sense of intimacy with the seemingly daunting structure. She allows us to see not only its finished splendor, but also the awkward growth phases that fed the curiosity or disdain of onlookers during construction. These non-judgmental yet insightful images document a unique episode in Seattle's history, and underscore our city's own efforts to grow and progress.

Through Swimmer's lens, the process of construction is an art form in itself. Myriad layers of scaffolding somehow forming a logical sequence, or scenes of workers perched at gravity-defying angles, confirm the visions of grandeur inherent in large civic projects, as well as the human investment required to make them happen.

Discerning and timely, this collection of images personalizes the building's struggle to emerge. It is a visual account of the passion, exertion, and expertise dedicated to the library's creation, as well as a lasting record of the construction technology that made it possible. Swimmer acquaints us with the stark beauty of this powerful new member of Seattle's architectural context, inspiring us to know more, and making the Seattle Central Library, as it should be, thoroughly accessible to all.

Bonnie Duncan, Architectural Writer

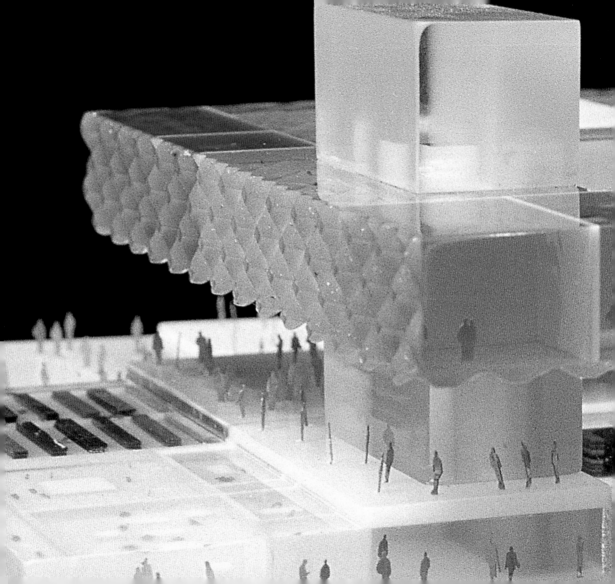

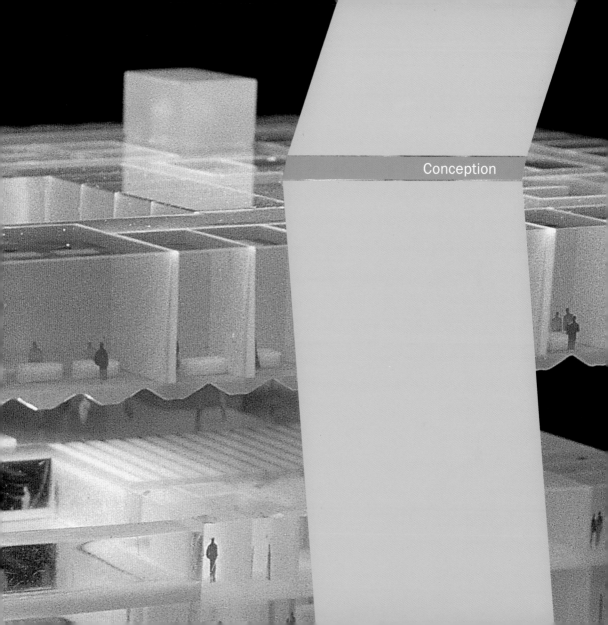

Conception

THE MODERN LIBRARY, ESPECIALLY IN A CYBER-CITY SUCH AS SEATTLE, MUST **TRANSFORM** ITSELF INTO AN INFORMATION STOREHOUSE AGGRESSIVELY ORCHESTRATING THE COEXISTENCE OF ALL AVAILABLE TECHNOLOGIES.

— *Rem Koolhaas, Partner OMA*

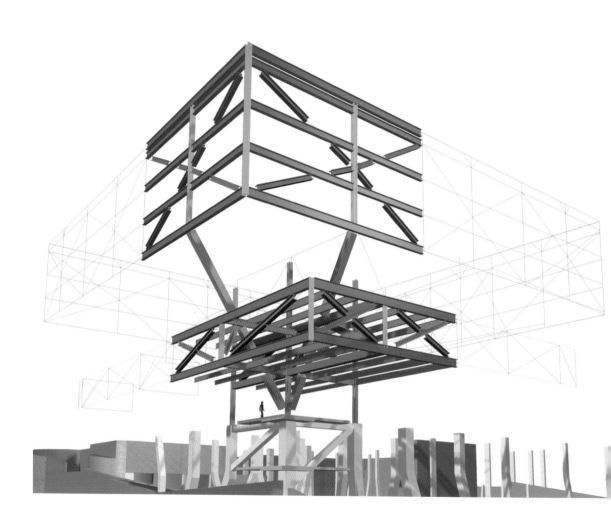

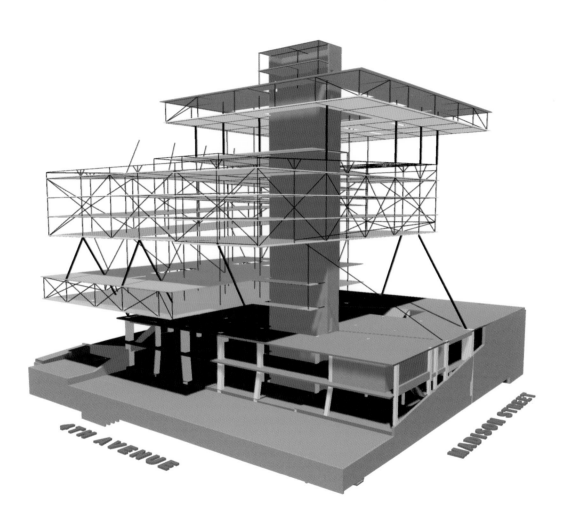

4TH AVENUE

MADISON STREET

Demolition

THE LIBRARY IS CAST AT THE VORTEX OF THE TWO MOST DRAMATIC CHANGES IN MODERN LIFE OVER THE LAST DECADE: THE **EROSION** OF THE PUBLIC REALM AND THE **EXPLOSION** OF NEW TECHNOLOGIES.

— *Sheri Olson, AIA, Architecture Critic*

Process

02-04-03

04-08-03

05-23-03

12-03-03

07-02-02

08-20-02

10-22-02

02-13-03

03-14-03

04-08-03

09-04-03

09-25-03

10-31-03

4-02   12-18-02   02-04-03

1-03   06-17-03   07-08-03

3-03   01-12-04   02-18-04

Steel & Glass

THE STRUCTURAL APPROACH WAS REALLY LIBERATING. FEW **COLUMNS** ARE VERTICAL. HOWEVER, WHERE COLUMNS ARE NOT VERTICAL, THEY ARE SLOPED OR **SKEWED** IN THE MOST DIRECT WAY TO SUPPORT THE **TRANSITION** BETWEEN WHERE A LOAD IS APPLIED AND WHERE IT IS BEST RESISTED.

— *Jay Taylor, Principal Engineer, Magnusson Klemencic Associates*

THE CURTAIN WALL, A SYSTEM OF GLASS PANES AND ALUMINUM MULLION GRID, HAS TO BE ABLE TO ACCOMMODATE TEMPERATURE, WIND, AND EARTHQUAKE MOVEMENTS. IT IS LIKE THE RELATIONSHIP OF **SKIN TO BODY**.

— *Andreas Zoch, Project Manager, Seele*

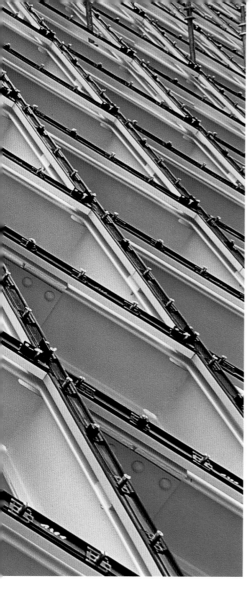

Spaces

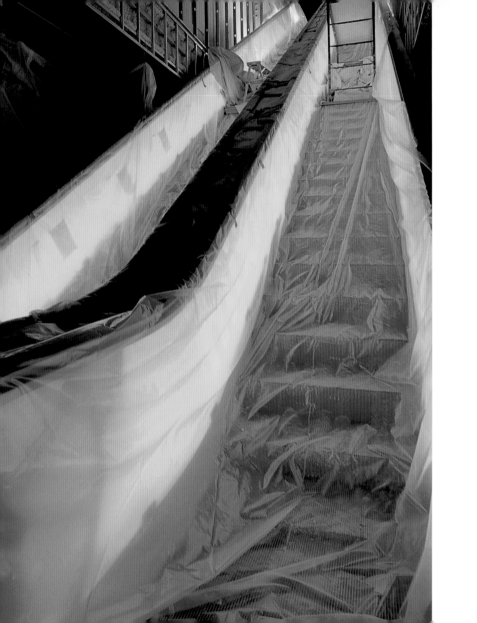

DOES A PUBLIC BUILDING HAVE A FAÇADE IN THE AGE OF ELECTRONICS? THE FACE HAS GIVEN WAY TO A KIND OF **INTERFACE**...IN WHICH ACTIVITIES ARE INSERTED AND HYPER-ENERGIZED.

— *Ayad Rahmani, Prof. of Architecture, Washington State University*

Transition

THERE IS A RELENTLESS INTERPLAY BETWEEN VARIOUS MATERIAL ELEMENTS OF THE BUILDING. THE FAÇADE BECOMES INTERIOR ARCHITECTURAL SPACE, AND MUCH OF THE STRUCTURAL SYSTEM IS EXPOSED AS A FINISHED PRODUCT. THIS INTENSE LEVEL OF **INTEGRATION** WAS A REAL CHALLENGE WITH REGARD TO CONSTRUCTION SEQUENCING.

— *Dale Stenning, Hoffman Construction, Washington*

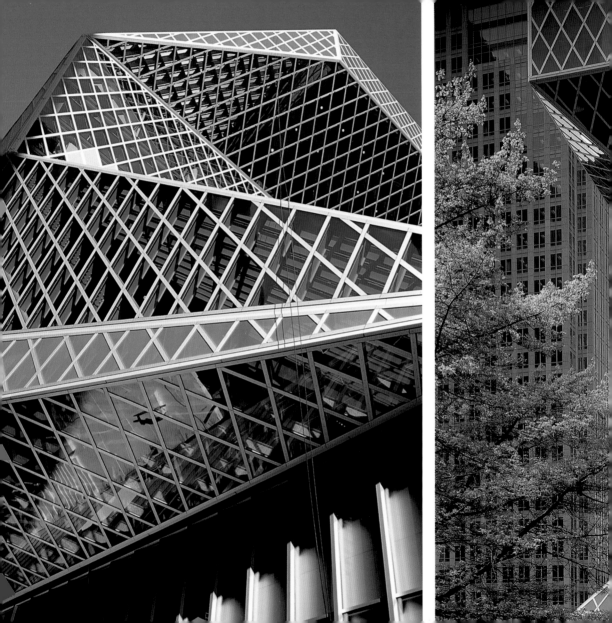

THE **SPIRAL** IS A CONTAINED WAREHOUSE FOR UP TO ONE MILLION BOOKS, ORGANIZED ON TERRACES AND MADE CONTIGUOUS BY HUNDREDS OF MINI-RAMPS THAT DOUBLE AS A FLEXIBLE IDENTIFICATION SYSTEM, GUARANTEEING THE **LEGIBILITY** OF THE COLLECTION AND MAKING IT A MODEL OF ACCESSIBILITY.

— *Robert Zimmer, Project Director, Design, LMN Architects*

CREDITS
p.8-9, 11 Resin model designed by OMA, courtesy Seattle Public Library.

p.10 Rem Koolhaas (partner OMA) quoted by Sheri Olson in "How Seattle Learned to Stop Worrying and Love Rem Koolhaas' Plans for a New Central Library," *Architectural Record* 188 (Aug. 2000): 121.

p.12-13 CAD renderings created by Magnusson Klemencic Associates, courtesy MKA.

p.18 Sheri Olson, AIA (architecture critic), "How Seattle Learned to Stop Worrying and Love Rem Koolhaas' Plans for a New Central Library," *Architectural Record* 188 (Aug. 2000): 121. Quote modified with permission from author.

p.36 Jay Taylor (principal engineer, MKA), Interview with Lara Swimmer, March 18, 2004.

p.44 Andreas Zoch (project manager, Seele, glass manufacturer), Interview with Lara Swimmer, March 29, 2004.

p.60 Ayad Rahmani (professor of architecture, Washington State University), "Library as Carnival," *ARCADE* 19 (Winter 2000): 26. Quote modified with permission from author.

p.68 Dale Stenning (project engineer, Hoffman Construction), Interview with Lara Swimmer, April 28, 2004.

p.70 Artist Ann Hamilton's "LEW Wood Floor."

p.74 Robert Zimmer (project director, design, LMN Architects), May 15, 2004.

p.79 Photo: Bart Eberwein

ACKNOWLEDGMENTS
Thank you to: **Robert Zimmer**, my partner and critic, for his knowledge, insight, advice, and support on this project and in general; **Venkat Balasubramani** for his legal counsel and friendship; **Jodee Fenton** for her enthusiasm; **Hoffman Construction** for its long-term support of my work; and my collaborators **Kurt Wolken** and **Petyr Beck**, for their excellent work in the design and editing realms.

I would like to express my truest appreciation to the **architects at OMA and LMN** for their craft, design, and vision in the creation of a brilliant and inspiring building, which served as impetus and muse for the photo exploration that is this book.

BIOGRAPHY

Lara Swimmer has spent the past 10 years documenting many of the Puget Sound area's most significant civic building projects, through construction and as finished monuments. Beginning with the Paramount Theatre's renovation in the early 1990s, she went on to photograph the Seattle Symphony's Benaroya Hall, renovation works at KeyArena, Cinerama, Union Station, and SODO Center, and new construction of Safeco Field, the Experience Music Project, and the Tacoma and Bellevue Art Museums. She also spent time photographing the Disney Concert Hall in Los Angeles.

In documenting the new downtown Seattle Public Library, Lara was influenced in part by her background as a student of film and critical theory. She now travels around the country for editorial assignments, and tries to return to Berlin every year to check in on the progress of the city where she first discovered architecture.